WWW

Willy's Wednesday Wisdom
2020–2021

W͟ILLIAM H͟ENRY M͟EYER

Fulton Books
Meadville, PA

Published by Fulton Books 2022

ISBN 978-1-63860-570-6 (paperback)
ISBN 978-1-63860-571-3 (digital)

Printed in the United States of America

CONTENTS

WWW 1

Copyright..2

Contents 3

Introduction..5

Dedication 7

Slices of Wisdom..9

Looking Forward..65

INTRODUCTION

There have been hundreds of books written with endless jokes and quotes. Many of those books list every quotation ever said or heard or written, regardless of relevance and message—whether it is good or bad, pertinent and timely—or just a Dictionary of quotes. I look upon a quotation in this book as a relevant and understandable representation of my thoughts. I've included my own "Quotes" and "Expanded Quotes," but I also borrowed quotes from others, giving credit to the writer when that information was known. In many cases, I've added my own little personalization, or twist, to the quote's presentation to make it more relevant to your everyday life. Consider the Quote from Wednesday, Mar 10, 2020.

"You know…I'm Worth It."

Or my "Expanded Quote" to add a touch of relevance.

> You know, it might be well to remind ourselves as we look in the mirror each morning to comb our hair or shave and say to ourselves, "You know…I'm Worth It."

This Is not a book of endless and boring Jokes or quotes. I think that this little book needs to be read once and then reread and then set on your nightstand. It is not a book to "Speed read" and then put on your bookshelf. Take a highlighter and highlight the slice of wisdom that may have a special interest to you. I keep my highlighter handy for daily thoughts that I may want to revisit.

So thanks for sampling and, hopefully, reading the rest of my short book. The book Is called WWW for "Willy's Wednesday Wisdom" for 2020–2021. One year of wisdom, or "Slices of Wisdom," and would you believe, a short (52 + 1) Wednesday's (52 + 1 pages). My entries are not always apparent or obvious, but as you process them, you may be reminded of a mindful relationship with them in your life. I do know that I have gone back to certain Wednesdays and revisited a thought, a slice of wisdom, at other times.

Perhaps you will find a message that you may relate to you in your everyday challenges and then allow you to assimilate that spark into a new mindset for your life going forward. It seems that we've fallen into the pattern of reading or hearing so much instant information and then just as quickly retreat to instant dismissal of what you just heard or read. There's always more Information bombarding you to take your mind off what you hear. So muse a bit, process a bit, keep the best and leave the rest.

The simple process of being mindful of the existence and search for these bits of wisdom has been invigorating for me. I've done this for a year now, and I have developed a new habit. I know I'll carry this habit forward into a new year, in my search of wisdom and relevance, and continue to seek out relevant slices of wisdom for my own personal life's journey.

We will all remember—and will not forget—this last year with the COVID-19 Virus and the effect that it had on all our lives, how it short-changed our lives. We secluded ourselves in our homes, but the mind never rests; it just adjusts in different ways, in different people.

Seclusion brings out different thinking in different people. It brought something out In me as I immersed myself in WWW. I hope that you might glean a personal insight in at least a few of the offerings that follow.

I have cited the original authors of the quotes that I have included in this book when they have been known to me. Other quotes of similar meaning or message have certainly been around the block before, but I have not purposely denied recognition of the original authors when I cite or paraphrase or adapt each message to my thoughts.

Thank you to all past authors that have given us such a storehouse of wisdom.

William Henry Meyer

DEDICATION

I started a year ago writing down some of my more mindful thoughts. I eventually put those thoughts—wisdom, if you will—into a weekly email and sent it to my family and friends. I called it "Willy's Wednesday Wisdom" or "WWW." I so appreciated my family and friends who responded in kind, with their questions, interpretations, or suggestions or an expanded thought on the "Slice of Wisdom" subject that I presented. Some even indicated an anticipation of what message might come to them, on the next Wednesday.

I, therefore, dedicate this book to my Family and Friends.

SLICES of WISDOM

SLICES OF WISDOM

Wednesday Apr 1, 2020   April Fool.................................12
Wednesday Apr 8, 2020   Who am I?..............................13
Wednesday Apr 15, 2020   Is It Over Yet? 14
Wednesday Apr 22, 2020   Soar High...............................15
Wednesday Apr 29, 2020   Your Path 16
Wednesday May 6, 2020   Your Spark 17
Wednesday May 13, 2020   Where Have You Been?..............18
Wednesday May 20, 2020   Changes! 19
Wednesday May 27, 2020   Add It Up 20
Wednesday Jun 3, 2020   What Day Is It?........................21
Wednesday Jun 10, 2020   Today 22
Wednesday Jun 17, 2020   And Don't Forget….....................23
Wednesday Jun 24, 2020   Hey! 24
Wednesday Jul 1, 2020   What Is Life?............................25
Wednesday Jul 8, 2020   Your Life..................................26
Wednesday Jul 15, 2020   Why?......................................27
Wednesday Jul 22, 2020   Smiles.....................................28
Wednesday Jul 29, 2020   Trees......................................29
Wednesday Aug 5, 2020   Lest You Forget 30
Wednesday Aug 12, 2020   Let Us Remember 31
Wednesday Aug 19, 2020   Till We Meet Again..................32
Wednesday Aug 26, 2020   Is it Really?.............................33
Wednesday Sep 2, 2020   Long Ago 34
Wednesday Sep 9, 2020   Be Resourceful. 35
Wednesday Sep 16, 2020   Your Journey 36
Wednesday Sep 23, 2020   What Do You See? 37
Wednesday Sep 30, 2020   How Old?................................38
Wednesday Oct 7, 2020   Create It..................................39

Wednesday Oct 14, 2020	*The Chase*	40
Wednesday Oct 21, 2020	*Change*	41
Wednesday Oct 28, 2020	*That Old Carpenter*	42
Wednesday Nov 4, 2020	*Carpenter's Rerun*	43
Wednesday Nov 11, 2020	*RSVPs*	44
Wednesday Nov 18, 2020	*Life's Time*	45
Wednesday Nov 25, 2020	*Predictions*	46
Wednesday Dec 2, 2020	*Your Company*	47
Wednesday Dec 9, 2020	*Today's Moment*	48
Wednesday Dec 16, 2020	*Attitude*	49
Wednesday Dec 23, 2020	*Life—What Is It?*	50
Wednesday Dec 30, 2020	*Kindness*	51
Wednesday Jan 6, 2021	*Your Thought*	52
Wednesday Jan 13, 2021	*More Thoughts*	53
Wednesday Jan 20, 2021	*Wants or Needs?*	54
Wednesday Jan 27, 2021	*Taste of Life*	55
Wednesday Feb 3, 2021	*Pandemic*	56
Wednesday Feb 10, 2021	*How to Be*	57
Wednesday Feb 17, 2021	*Secrets*	58
Wednesday Feb 24, 2021	*What Do You Know?*	59
Wednesday Mar 3, 2021	*Chapters of Life*	60
Wednesday Mar 10, 2021	*Your Worth*	61
Wednesday Mar 17, 2021	*Impressions*	62
Wednesday Mar 24, 2021	*Wisdom*	63
Wednesday Mar 31, 2021	*Anniversary*	64

Wednesday Apr 1, 2020

"April Fool"

No—Seriously—a journey of mindful quotes.
Today—May I start on a new journey of borrowed wisdom
along with some of my own personal life lessons and reflections.
I may be "Crazy," but
Join me for the inauguration of
"Willy's Wednesday Wisdom."

Wednesday Apr 8, 2020

Who am I?

Be yourself—everyone else is already taken.
—Oscar Wilde

Yes, it might be well to know who you really are.

Wednesday Apr 15, 2020

Is It Over Yet?

*Good News, but don't be impatient—be Mindful of
the Virus and that Baseball Game of Life.*

It ain't over till it's over.
                                        —Yogi Berra

Wednesday Apr 22, 2020

Soar High

*Don't ever underestimate who you are and
what you can do—remember that.*

*No bird soars too high if he soars
with his own wings.*

—William Blake

Your Path

*If you find a path with no obstacles, it
probably doesn't lead anywhere.*
—*Frank A. Clark*

*But keep walking—or you won't have the opportunity
to even find a path, or make a choice.*

Wednesday May 6, 2020

Your Spark

"Nurture that spark within you and you will find a bonfire."

Wednesday May 13, 2020

Where Have You Been?

I was having a great day until I woke up.
—Richard Lewis

On the other hand...
—Tevye the Dairyman

Each new day—to me—is a new discovery.
I've never been there before.

Wednesday May 20, 2020

Changes!

"Be mindful as to whether you are evolving or just going around in circles" For which you might prescribe...

"Nothing Changes if Nothing Changes."

Wednesday May 27, 2020

Add It Up

In the spirit and verity of my Wednesday offerings,
I am proud of the facticity of all my messages, so in this spirit, and my
erudite display of superior intellect, I am proud to offer the following:

Did you know that 97% of the world is dumb?
Luckily I'm in the other 5%.
—Danny Jackson

Wednesday Jun 3, 2020

What Day Is It?

"Don't forget your yesterdays and don't deny yourself your tomorrows but be mindful that 'today' is the best day of them all."

Wednesday Jun 10, 2020

Today

"Remember to live your life today—'tomorrow' never comes."

Wednesday Jun 17, 2020

And Don't Forget...

*If you don't know where you are going,
you might end up someplace else.*

—Yogi **Berra**

Wednesday Jun 24, 2020

Hey!

"Stop solving problems that you don't have"
OR to say it in another way
"If it ain't broke, don't fix it."

Wednesday Jul 1, 2020

What Is Life?

This week I am mindful of the Life and Love that
Lucy and I shared together but ended one year ago—Jun 29, 2019.
Remember that...
Life Is made up of Joys and Sorrows,
Life is made up of "Little Moments,"
Life always has Its Turning Points,
Life becomes a thread of "Happenings,"
Life defines your "Moral Compass."

Your life can be rough—or it can be great.
It all depends on whether we approach it with the "Right Attitude."

So live your life with optimism with what's ahead,
not on satisfaction with what's behind.

Wednesday Jul 8, 2020

Your Life

*"Live your life as if it was a three-legged stool.
It will always be steady.
Call those legs Wisdom, Love, and Humor."*

Why?

*Why are segments of America and the World so swift to harm others?
There is a universal Maxim that is recognized by the major world
religions (and nonreligions) which is so contrary to this mindset.
It's called the "Golden Rule" stated in many different
words, but all with the same meaning, i.e.*

Ancient Egypt:
"That which you hate to be done to you, do not do to another."

Ancient Greece:
"Do not do to others that which angers you when they do it to you."

Ancient Rome:
"Treat your inferior as you would wish your superior to treat you."

Judaism:
*"You shall not take vengeance or bear a grudge against your kinsfolk.
Love your neighbor as yourself."*

Christianity:
"Do to others what you want them to do to you."

Hinduism:
*"One should never do that to another which one
regards as injurious to one's own self."*

Buddhism:
"Hurt not others in ways that you yourself would find hurtful."

Or as commonly written...
"Do unto others as you would have them do unto you."

Borrowed from—and credit to—Wikipedia

Wednesday Jul 22, 2020

Smiles

HEY, you all know—by now—that I'm into "Smiles."
There are hundreds of languages in the world, but a
Smile speaks all of them, and also remember...

Smiles are free so share them.
                    —Michelle F. Florida

"Don't let your Smiles stay in a box—unwrap
the box—and wear them proudly."

Wednesday Jul 29, 2020

Trees

*Be mindful, the next time you sit under that
large, beautiful, leafy shade tree that…*

*Someone's sitting in the shade today because
someone planted a tree a long time ago.*
—*Warren Buffet*

*You are that person under the tree, the tree, as Joyce
Kilmer has opined, "only God can make a tree."
But—may I add—we are here to plant them.*

Wednesday Aug 5, 2020

Lest You Forget

I am what I am, and that's all that I am.
*—**Popeye***

BUT—also remember to
Never lose your perspective.
Remember "Bullshit" is a necessity to a bull.

Let Us Remember

Some of the simple but oft-forgotten responsibilities
of being a member of the human race.
Let us be mindful of the guiding elements of…

"gemutlichkeit" (German for coziness and friendship)
"camaraderie" (a spirit of good fellowship)
Wisdom | Love | Humor | Generosity | Empathy | Tolerance | Respect
| Diversity | Compassion | Compromise | Sharing | Patience

There is no room for anything less in the future of this
shrinking world and the survival of mankind.

Wednesday Aug 19, 2020

Till We Meet Again

We are all visitors in this world of ours—some of us stay longer,
some of us stay less. We have just lost one of us that stayed less.
So, in this mindset, let us reflect—in the context of the sailors
in our family—that as we watch Nic's ship, as it disappears
over the horizon, and say "There he goes," be mindful that—
on the other side—we may also say "Here he comes."

These words—of course—are from that comforting poem by
Luther F. Beecher, "Gone from My Sight."

So, let us all say to Nic—Godspeed on your journey—and let
us cherish, those of us, that are still visitors "on this side."

Is it Really?

You all know that new phrase that is going around.
I've caught myself using it…
"It is what it is."
BUT—on reflection—it's dead wrong; it's a cop-out: "It just ain't right."
We have an obligation to ourselves, and to others, to not accept the
status quo: the easy answer. We need to listen, to observe, to process
new ideas and events and discard them or make them better.
You all know the other old cop-out…
"If you hear a lie often enough, you begin to accept it as the truth."
That certainly "ain't right" either.

SO use the mind that God gave you—take that harder—
but right path and reject the lazy conclusion that…
"It is what it is."

Long Ago

May we consider two quotes from my long-ago past.

There's so much good in the worst of us and
so much bad in the best of us, that it hardly
behooves any of us, to talk about the rest of us.
*　　　　　—my Fifth-Grade Teacher*

If you can't say something nice about
someone, don't say anything.
*　　　　—Grandmas and Moms everywhere*

Wednesday Sep 9, 2020

Be Resourceful.

Always remember to...
Do what you can,
With what you have,
Where you are.
We really have more than we think.

Wednesday Sep 16, 2020

Your Journey

The journey is the reward.
                              —*Tao Saying*

Listen to your inner music and enjoy…

"A Taste of Honey"

Wednesday Sep 23, 2020

What Do You See?

*There is so much magic and awe in the world all
around us—may we be mindful of our senses.
It's not what you look at that
matters, it's what you see.*
                    —Henry David Thoreau

*Or perhaps a corollary or two…
"It's not what you touch that matters, it's what you feel."
"It's not what you listen to, it's what you hear."*

Wednesday Sep 30, 2020

How Old?

Your Age is only a number—wisdom is ageless.
Aging brings about physical changes—it always happens.
***But**...Beauty is in your "being" more than in your "looks."*

Remember again our friend Mark Twain when he says,
"Wrinkles should merely indicate where Smiles have been."

***So** "If you have the right attitude, you will*
change, but... You will never grow old."

Wednesday Oct 7, 2020

Create It

Don't wait for the right opportunity: create it.
—George Bernard Shaw

Wednesday Oct 14, 2020

The Chase

Never chase Love, Affection, or Attention. If it isn't given freely by another person, it isn't worth having.

Wednesday Oct 21, 2020

Change

Always Remember…
"Nothing changes if nothing changes."

Wednesday Oct 28, 2020

That Old Carpenter

*It might be well to revisit that old carpenter's
axiom that reminds us to...*
"measure twice—cut once" with a new twist and
"think twice—speak once."

Wednesday Nov 4, 2020

Carpenter's Rerun

Last week, the carpenters improved my speaking habits.
Perhaps they can help me with the following this week.
> *Think Less, Feel More,*
> *Frown Less, Smile More,*
> *Talk Less, Listen More,*
> *Judge Less, Accept More,*
> *Watch Less, Do More,*
> *Complain Less, Appreciate More,*
> *Fear Less, Love More.*

Wednesday Nov 11, 2020

RSVPs

I had a "Wine and Cheese" Party today...
I didn't invite anyone.
No one came!

Life's Time

Life is available only in the present moment.
—Thich Nhat Hanh

So experience your life in every moment that you have.

Wednesday Nov 25, 2020

Predictions

Predictions are difficult, especially about the future.
—Yogi Berra

Wednesday Dec 2, 2020

Your Company

Never accept your own company as second best.
—Sally Alter

It will be with you for the rest of your life.

Wednesday Dec 9, 2020

Today's Moment

*There will be many opportunities for wonderful
"moments" awaiting you this day.
How will you respond to them?*

Wednesday Dec 16, 2020

Attitude

*"Life can be rough or life can be sweet…
if we approach life, with the right attitude."*

Wednesday Dec 23, 2020

Life—What Is It?

Have you ever pondered a typical response to…
"How's your Life?" with the probable answer?
I guess it's okay—I lead a "normal" life.
I thought about that and analogized it and concluded that…
"my car doesn't go very far in 'neutral' gear."

Wednesday Dec 30, 2020

Kindness

*The smallest act of kindness is worth
more than the grandest intention.*

—Oscar Wilde

*It has also been said that…
The nicest things come in small packages.*

Wednesday Jan 6, 2021

Your Thought

Muse on this message a bit but don't ask me for an explanation.
"A good thought is not always a· good· idea."

Wednesday Jan 13, 2021

More Thoughts

*I liked the corollary that was offered in response
to my last week's muse…to repeat it here.*

Too much of a good thing is better.

*And may I add a further observation:
"Too little of a bad thing is too much."*

Wednesday Jan 20, 2021

Wants or Needs?

As we continue in our individual quests to accumulate stuff, let us be mindful of our purpose... Is It "needed" or just "wanted"? Do we get things because we just "want" them...or Do we get things because we truly "need" them?

Wednesday Jan 27, 2021

Taste of Life

Thank you for joining me for… "Willy's Wednesday Wisdom" and a taste of life in three little words: "Live, Love, Laugh."

Wednesday Feb 3, 2021

Pandemic

COVID-19: They say, "An ounce of prevention
is worth a pound of cure."
How great has medical science been to us by
giving each of us an ounce of gold?

I gratefully offered my arm to be punctured with a needle on
Jan 29 to perhaps give me "prevention" in lieu of a pound of
"cure" that—if once infected by this killer virus—a cure,
I might never even have the opportunity to see.
SO...I'll be ready on Feb 26 for that reassuring second needle.

How to Be

Ben Franklin puts it this way:
Be civil to all, Sociable to many,
Familiar with few, Friend to one,
Enemy to none.

However, my friends and I are musing about
the validity of "Friend to one."

Wednesday Feb 17, 2021

Secrets

"A secret is no longer a secret when you tell it to only one other person."
How true this is.

What Do You Know?

After many, many years,
I finally realized that I didn't know everything.
BUT…"On the other hand" (Tevye)
I also realized that…
"I know what I know."

Wednesday Mar 3, 2021

Chapters of Life

Childhood, Teens, 20s, 30s, 40s, 50s, 60s, 70s, 80s, 90s?
Each chapter brings joyful memories (and some sad ones too).
BUT Wherever you are in your book of life,
remember, "the best is yet to come."
And so in the appropriate perspective of Yogi Berra.

It ain't over till it's over.

—Yogi Berra

Your Worth

You know, it might be well to remind ourselves, as we look in the mirror each morning, to comb our hair, or shave, and say to ourselves, "You know…I'm worth it."

Wednesday Mar 17, 2021

Impressions

Happy St. Pat's Day
As we leave a very trying year behind us and as we
start to get "out and about" again meeting people, it
might be well to be reminded of this old maxim:
"You don't get a second chance to make a first impression."

Wisdom

They have said, "Gold is where you find It."
I might also say, "Wisdom is where you find It."

You all know that your future has been destined—before—by the "Fortune Cookie." Recently I found wisdom in an individually wrapped piece of chocolate. It was written on the inside of the crumpled wrapper, but if you took the time to unfold the wrapping carefully so it wouldn't tear, you would have found this thought on directing your life...

When life isn't going right, go left.
—Haylea S. in South Dakota

Wednesday Mar 31, 2021

Anniversary

*Would you believe that "Willy's Wednesday
Wisdom" is one year old today so…
I'm celebrating its anniversary.
When—on Apr 1, 2020—I started this little diversion, I
never thought that I was so full of it (wisdom, that Is) that I
could go on, and last, for a year. But I did—and here I am.
I've even got a few more Ideas archived that I haven't used
up, so my folly will continue for a while longer in 2021.*

LOOKING FORWARD

So what's next? I have already opined that I've still got some unused thoughts for next year.

I realized that I have settled into a new habit, this last year, 2020–2021, of being more mindful of what I hear, of what I read, of what I think. Each past Wednesday for a year, I have encouraged myself, disciplined myself, to put down on paper some thought that emerged, from what I had observed, during the week. Thus, my "Willy's Wednesday Wisdom" began not on Jan 1, when the year starts, but on April 1 when something totally unexpected occurred—the realization of a world pandemic was upon us. Maybe this was an April Fool's Joke on myself, but by April of 2020, our country, our world, was in the eye of the storm of COVID-19. It was uncontrolled. We were asked to limit our normal daily activities, to stay away from people (What?), to stay home.

Try to take a mouthful, as we all did, of that exercise in seclusion of mindfulness. (Or was it mindlessness?)

So, stay at home, be mindful, don't gather with others…find a diversion…start a collection of mindful thoughts—of wisdom—of reading between the lines of news. I decided on "Willy's Wednesday Wisdom" to identify my frustration, look for good thoughts, self-awareness thoughts, identify some stupid maxims going around.

There are books written on great remarks made by great thoughtful people (i.e., Mark Twain, Henry Thoreau, Chinese Philosophers, American Icons, Yogi Berra, Henry Ford, etc.). There are also interesting thoughts on candy wrappers and in Fortune Cookies. Wisdom Is surely wherever you find it. There are long books of quotations that offer every quotation the author has accumulated. Some are very perceptive; many are really bad. You, as reader, are forced to take the best and leave the rest. I wanted to be more selective with my own quotes, as well as In the quotes of others that I selected. It fits me. I hope it fits you.

Well, what should I call my little exercise in wisdom? My name is William. (How about Willy?)

Wednesday is a day, but Wednesday is also known as the "Hump Day" of the week, the middle day, the fourth day of the week, the day of the week that you need to decide. Is this day the "end of the beginning" or the "beginning of the end" of this current week? (You decide.)

Thoughts to remember—could they be called "Wisdom"? I am certainly old enough to have some so-called wisdom thoughts—why not?

So I'll call It (and I did) "Willy's Wednesday Wisdom" or conveniently condensed to "WWW."

Have a Happy Life and keep your creative and mindful persuasions at the forefront.

William Henry Meyer

CPSIA information can be obtained
at www.ICGtesting.com
Printed in the USA
BVHW082301081122
651445BV00006B/451

9 781638 605706